Content Marketing
How to Build a Great Brand and Gain High Loyalty Customer

Table of Contents

Introduction 4

Chapter 1 – What Is Content Marketing? 5

What Makes It Different? 6
What Can It Do For Your Audience? 8
The Key Advantages 9
What Makes It Better Than Copywriting? 11

Chapter 2 – Preparing Your Content 13

Develop a Mission Statement 13
Understanding Your Audience 14
Schedule An Interview 15
Figure Out Your Goals 17

Chapter 3 – Choosing Your Content 19

Setting Up a Smarter Strategy 19
What Unique Things Are There? 21
What Do You Understand? 22
Pay Attention To Trends 22
Search For Keywords 24
Prepare Categories 24
Brainstorming 25
Don't Develop Too Much 27

Chapter 4 – Laying Out Your Data Right 29

Four Basic Parts 29
Use Fewer Words At a Time 31

Give People a Sense Of What You Do Early 32

Set Up Connections 32

Be To the Point 33

Create Visual Representations 33

Adding Pictures 35

Chapter 5 – Marketing Avenues 37

Website 37

Blogging 38

Direct Mail 39

Social Media 40

Sharing Images 42

Using Email the Right Way 43

Chapter 6 – Key Pointers For Marketing 45

Understand Your Audience 45

Focus On One Channel At a Time 46

Keep a Smart Schedule 46

Chapter 7 – Creating a Call to Action 48

Don't Forget Social Sharing Buttons 50

Chapter 8 – Additional Tips 52

Place a Local Focus 52

Reply To Messages Often 53

Think About Search Intentions 54

Use Analytics Programs 54

Conclusion 56

Introduction

The concept of content marketing is not something that many people think about but it's one that can make a difference when you're trying to let others know about what you have to offer. Content marketing will help you establish your company's brand as you grow your business. More importantly, it helps you to show the world what makes your business different from everyone else.

This guide will help you understand what makes content marketing a noteworthy practice for your business' use. You will learn about how content marketing will help you to create a stronger image for your business and how to make it a more efficient and sensible solution for your marketing demands.

The focus of content marketing entails creating promotional materials that are different from what you might see elsewhere. A great marketing campaign is no longer about only telling people who you are and what it is you have to offer. It's also about sharing content that is relevant to your goals and is especially valuable. It's about showing that you know more about what you have to offer, thus making your business more appealing to the average reader.

You will see what you can do when trying to create content and how to organize it right. This includes knowing where to send your content out to, how to probe your audience and much more.

After reading this guide, you should have a better idea of how to make content marketing work for you. You might be amazed at how well your plans can work if used well enough.

Content is king in today's marketing world. You will learn all about how to make content work to your advantage right through this convenient and useful guide.

Chapter 1 – What Is Content Marketing?

To get a clear picture of what makes content marketing so advantageous for your business, you have to take a closer look at what it is in general. It is a popular practice that makes businesses noticeable and easier to benefit from.

Content marketing is a practice where you will create free content that can be used by all kinds of people. You will take your content and send it out to people who might be likely to do business with you.

This content can include a variety of things. It can include articles that relate to your business' functions or what you have to sell. Videos that showcase you in action or details on what's available will certainly help. You can even take pictures and share them with other people.
The content can go on social media sites or blogs. It can even go onto flyers that you can send to people through a traditional mail service. You will have the freedom to do what you feel with your content as you see fit.
The key here is that the content is unique and specific to your business. It is something that you will more than likely have created on your own although you always have the option of using someone else's content if needed.
The content that you will offer will be related to what you are selling. You are essentially educating people about whatever it is you have to offer and what makes what you have so valuable and appealing to everyone.

What Makes It Different?

Content marketing is clearly different from traditional marketing on the basis that you're making your message more unique. It will be specific to your business instead of just being something that is far too generic in its style.

The key part of content marketing is that it will establish a message that your target audience will clearly understand. By using content marketing, you will do more than just let someone know about what you have to offer. You will also show people that you understand whatever it is you want to share.
Let's take a look at a few things that make content marketing so unique.
1. It shares details on the experience you are trying to provide.

Telling people about what your business offers can make a difference. However, you have to share details on whatever experience might be felt when you're marketing your work.
The experience that you are selling will entail something relating to how you will use your work to your advantage. You might share details on what you know about your work and how to make it different from what everyone else in the world has.
2. It shows that you want to get in touch with your audience.

Content marketing lets you share information with your audience in a manner that is sensible and unique. You will be sharing information based on what you feel your readers might be interested in above all else. This in turn gives you more control over how you're going to share information with other people.

3. Your business will also use its own system for telling people things.

The problem with many forms of marketing is that they often entail just sharing data that is too commonplace and similar. That is, you might end up sharing content that is close to identical to whatever you want to share.
Content marketing is truly unique in terms of how you're going to market yourself. You'd going to do more than just post your name out there. You'll let people understand what you know and that your business is a trustworthy one.

What Can It Do For Your Audience?

Content marketing can be advantageous for your business as it does many things for your audience. In particular, content marketing can do the following:

- It helps you acquire new customers by sharing more details on what makes your business stand out.

- You will also retain the existing customers that you hold. You will remind them of how knowledgeable you are about your field.

- It also makes people more aware of what your business does in general. Instead of just focusing on just telling people you exist, you will also showcase what you know.

- You will also establish a sense of trust with anyone you're getting in touch with. You will show everyone that you clearly know what makes your business function the right way.

This practice will certainly do well for when you're trying to make your business visible. But there is more to content marketing than just these particular features.

The Key Advantages

There are plenty of great advantages of content marketing that make it the ideal solution for your business' demands.

- Your website will get more content to work with. This content can be about anything you've got to highlight. This makes it so people will understand what you have to offer.

- Your website will be easier to spot on a search engine. Today's search engines reward sites based on how unique their content is and what makes it stand out.

- People will trust in your business when you use content marketing. They will know that there's substance behind what you have to offer.

- People will also refer your website to other people thanks to how you're sharing information with them. This in turn expands your reach well beyond just who you are targeting at the very start.

- Your brand's reputation will improve as you share your work with more people. This comes as people will start to notice that your brand is worthwhile and has a meaning to it.

- Your brand will also become more visible in general. This added support will help you do more when getting more out of your marketing campaign.

- This may also be more cost effective than other marketing options. This is thanks to how you're going to market your business with data that can be shared many times over. People can always forward that data to make it more appealing and useful.

What Makes It Better Than Copywriting?

It is true that copywriting can certainly be great for your use. Copywriting allows you to create new content. It can help you create great landing pages for your website or emails dedicated to driving conversions.

Content marketing is actually a better solution. It takes the principles of copywriting and expands upon it.

With content marketing, you will use videos, blogs, social media sites and other places to share content. You will draft your content and share it in more spots. This creates a more attractive organization that makes it to where your content will look and work well.

Content marketing takes your copywriting materials and makes them easier for people to read. It's even made to help you share your content as people can forward it on social media or email among other avenues. In fact, content marketing data is easier to forward than anything you create through a more traditional copywriting process.

You should think about how well content marketing can work wonders for your promotional demands. However, you have to ensure you choose the right content that is smart and useful if you want it to work for you. The next part of this guide is dedicated to helping you figure out what content you need to utilize.

Chapter 2 – Preparing Your Content

The first part of getting content marketing to work is to think about the foundation you will use when getting it ready. Your foundation for your content marketing plans can entail a setup that focuses heavily on what you want to say and do for your customers.

Develop a Mission Statement

The first thing to do when getting your content up and running is to establish a mission statement. This is the basic reason for why your project exists in the first place.

Your goal when developing a mission statement is to think about what you want to do for your customers and how you're going to communicate with them. There are three critical aspects of a mission statement that you must use:

1. The core audience that you are targeting must be considered. Think about the person who you feel will benefit from you the most.

2. Consider the types of information that you want to offer when making your content. This information to be delivered must be clearly defined.

3. The outcome that you want to get out of your audience must be added. This refers to what your audience will do after they have read your content.

When making this work, consider how you will inform people and what content you want to develop. Think about the plans you have make sure it's all based on the statement you make.

Understanding Your Audience

Your particular audience can make a difference in your content marketing campaign. This audience can be one that is more likely to want to use your products or services.
You must think about the audience you have based on who buys your products or services or who might be more likely to do this. By understanding whom will be targeted, you can craft a content marketing campaign that fits in well with the needs that you hold.
Take a look at information relating to your business based on who does it with you. Look at points like how people would buy or use services from your business and compare demographics if possible. Think about any localities you want to target as well.

You must look into the specifics of your audience. This lets you zero in on the particular audience you want to target. As a result, it should be easier for you to market your work to other people without looking too confusing or unusual as you are doing so.

The most important thing to do when figuring out your audience is to avoid trying to target everyone. This is regardless of whether or not you can find a reason to target every person.

By targeting a general audience, you are creating one big message for all people to follow. This message may not be consistent among all people. Some people might have no idea as to whatever it is you want to share because you're clearly not paying attention to the desires they have. In addition, you might be sending messages to certain people who aren't going to respond or even be aware of what you're doing.

Be careful when getting your audience figured out when getting your content ready. Your audience must be organized well enough to provide you with a clear idea of what you should be saying to all those people.

Schedule An Interview

A great idea for understanding your audience is to get an interview with someone you might target. You can do this a few times when preparing your marketing campaign.

An interview will be easy to follow if you use these steps:

1. Interview someone who has used your product or service before.

2. Make sure when choosing an interview subject that you find someone who is honest and willing to be truthful about what he or she thinks of you.

3. Keep the interview from going on for far too long. A good interview can go for about 30 minutes.

4. Talk with an interview subject about what he or she thinks about your business. Delve into as many aspects as possible.

5. Think about the problems that someone has more than the positives. You need to fix the issues first before you can start hyping up whatever it is someone really likes out of your business.

6. Ask about what someone thinks about when looking into whether or not your product is worth buying. This part helps you determine what can be done to fix an issue at hand.

7. Ask about what triggered a desire to take action. Sometimes it could be a special offer but in other cases it's a part of a product or service that someone really likes that can trigger it.

8. Talk about what someone found to be useful in the decision to buy something. Sometimes one or two specific points might guide a person into making a call on whether or not to buy something.

The interview can help you learn about what someone is thinking about. This in turn makes it to where you will have more of an idea of what you should be doing as you're drafting a great plan.

Figure Out Your Goals

Before you choose your content for your marketing plans, you have to think about the goals you have. These goals can entail anything but the key is to make it so people will notice what you have to offer.
For instance, you might have a goal to offer something special to people or to let them know about something new you have. You might also have a desire to convince people about something relating to your business.

The goals you could use are rather varied. Here's a look at a few of the different goals you can consider working with:

- You might want to raise awareness of your brand.

- You might need to get more leads for your business. These include leads you can gather through your email list.

- One goal can be to inform people about everything that your business has to offer.

- There may be a need to convince curious customers to take the next step and pay money for something you've got.

- A desire to retain customers can be important too. This goal is especially important if you have competition.

When done right, your business will have a very easy time with growing and succeeding. You might be amazed at what you can do for your content marketing plans if you just think about how it's going to work for your use.

Chapter 3 – Choosing Your Content

While you can always work with content marketing to make people understand the difference between your business and others, you have to think carefully when doing so. You should understand the content you are working with while making it easier to share with other people.

You must start when working with a content marketing plan by thinking about the content in particular that you want to highlight. The kind of content that you want to focus on could certainly vary based on a variety of points like what your business does or how your business will serve people and so forth.

You must choose the content you want to market the right way. There are many ways how you can figure out what you are going to market your business with so you will have an easier time with highlighting whatever your business has.

Setting Up a Smarter Strategy

You must start by looking into the strategy that you want to utilize. The strategy can entail a good arrangement to make it easier for you to manage your content the right way.

You must establish a strategy that focuses on figuring out what you want to share. There are plenty of things that can be done in your strategy:

- You can start by establishing a set brand that fits in well. This brand will relate to the image you want to establish and how it will be shared with other people.

- A particular persona must also be established. This part of the strategy can entail working hard to get your business to grow.

- A larger story must also be figured out. The story can entail a need to share information with people over time and to make the content work out well. This should be used properly with a sensible arrangement that is easy to understand while captivating your audience.

There are basic points for your strategy to use. Having a smarter setup that isn't too complicated or hard to use will certainly work well for your use. It is important for you to see what you can get out of this content and how it will work for you.

What Unique Things Are There?

You could always consider the unique things that make your business stand out when choosing the content you want to highlight. You must explain what makes your business special as you're marketing yourself.

Content marketing entails showing that you are different from everyone else. The content you post can highlight all sorts of things that make you special:

- Unique products or services you have to offer

- Details on any experience you have with something

- Any plans you have for the future in terms of growing or expanding

- Any guarantees you might use in some cases

What Do You Understand?

One of the greatest reasons why people use content marketing entails making it easier for others to understand content. You have to share content that you know is easy to figure out and isn't too complicated.

You must share information with other people if you have something special to tell them. You will be easier for people to trust in when you manage data that is sensible.

Think carefully before posting anything about what you want to share with other people. The key is to share information that isn't too hard to follow.

Pay Attention To Trends

The online world is always changing. There are many great trends popping up all the time with new trends relating to running a business always coming about. The trends that you might come across will vary and should be explored carefully to give yourself an idea of what you can get out of your work.

The trends that are out there include points relating to what keywords people are searching for. These trends can change due to a variety of events or occasions. Sometimes a seasonal need might cause trends to change; this is why you're likely to see Christmas-related trends near the end of the year.

Meanwhile, some trends might change based on news stories. New political trends or laws might cause trends for society in general to change.

Be on the lookout for whatever trends are coming about in the world. You might have to adjust the content for your work based on the types of trends that are out there right now.

Here are a few tips to use when working with trends:

- Set up an RSS feed from a service like Feedly to get information on trends as they come about.

- Use Google Alerts to get regular updates on how people are searching for certain trends. Try and stick with the trends that are relevant to your work.

- Keep tabs on what other leaders in your industry are doing. They might be just as influential as the trends that you come across. This is thanks to these leaders possibly following the trends that you want to follow.

Search For Keywords

A keyword search may help you figure out what content is more popular out there. You can perform a search through a prominent search engine like Google to get a clear idea of what you can get out of your work.

Your search can help you find keywords that are relevant to whatever you want to do with your project. As you use the right keywords, you will find that it won't be hard for you to make your project run right.

This search process can help you figure out what is right for your project. You can use this to figure out if you're using the best possible keywords for the task or if you need help in some other way.

Prepare Categories

Another point to use is to think carefully about the categories that you want to utilize. The categories that will be involved in your campaign will certainly make a difference.

You can always create categories to use as a means of interacting with your target audience. Your categories will work by helping sort out the bits of content that you want to focus on. By choosing the right categories for content, you can create a content marketing campaign that is based on ideas and subjects that you know will work properly.

Think about the vision you have for your company or the types of products or services you have to offer. Think about the different categories that might be established based on that work. See that the content is smart enough based on what you want to share and how that content will work. This could help you get more information out there.

If you have come up with enough content then you must think about the ideas you have come across to see what categories they fit in.

Brainstorming

The next consideration to see when coming up with content involves brainstorming. This is done to help you get a clear idea of what you might use in the event that you need help in some way.

Brainstorming is a very simple concept. It is one where you will take a closer look at what you can do to develop a better plan. Brainstorming works with a setup where you throw different ideas around and see what new things can come about out of them.

The ideas that can come out of the session will certainly vary based on what you use. You might be amazed at how your work will be a little more developed depending on what you come across.

There are many steps you can use when getting your brainstorming session up and running.

1. Select a particular topic that you want to work with.

2. Write down the topic on a piece of paper, chalkboard or other surface.

3. List as many things relating to that topic as you can. Don't worry if they aren't related all that closely to the initial idea.

4. Review what you have prepared on your list.

5. After coming across the best ideas that you have written, create some new ideas based on the best ones. This will narrow down the scope of what you want to share.

There should be no limits as to what you can add to your page. When used right, it should be easy for you to get the most out of your campaign. The best part is that it is not too hard for you to get new ideas coming about if you just spend a bit of time on the process.

Don't Develop Too Much

Developing an idea is great but the last thing you'd want to do is develop more than necessary. Overdevelopment is a serious problem that often gets the most of people. Overdevelopment occurs when you have looked into a single idea for far too long. It causes you to think far too much about one small topic. Even worse, overdevelopment makes it to where you won't have time to think about other topics. You will be stuck on one topic to the point where you can't think about whatever else you want to do.

You must balance your time between each bit of content in your marketing plan. Thinking about one idea above others and using enough control over different concepts is always good to consider doing.

Remember to look carefully when it comes to getting the content for your marketing plan ready. Your content marketing setup will certainly be perfect when you work hard enough.

Chapter 4 – Laying Out Your Data Right

The data that you're using when getting your content marketing campaign running can make a real difference. You must think about how you're using data to make it easier for your campaign to look its best.

The appearance of your content marketing campaign can make a real difference. It helps people to understand what you are doing while also helping you to establish a sense of organization. As it is used properly, you will find that it is not too hard for the campaign you establish to work right.

You must especially be careful as people will take the data you want to share seriously. They want to see that you actually understand whatever it is you are talking about.

Four Basic Parts

Your data must be kept organized when you're marketing things to people. This is to keep things from being complicated. More importantly, it guides you through the process of creating something sensible and unique. There are four parts in your content marketing campaign that must be used every time:
1. An Introduction

The introduction will help people learn more about what you have to offer and what makes it special. It gathers someone's attention and lets someone know about what you want to say.

2. A Body

The body will cover whatever you introduced but in more detail. It is typically longer than the other sections but it does explain everything to your reader.

You need at least three details that can support your content. Three details proves that you have enough content to work with and that you understand whatever it is you want to share.

3. A Closing

The closing section will bring you from the body to the introduction again. It ties together what you said in the body with what you promised in the introduction.

You can always add something relating to how what you wrote about benefits the reader. This reinforces the need to stick with your work for whatever purpose you hold.

4. A Call to Action

The call to action is where you tell someone what that person should do after reading. This call may entail going to a website to buy a product or to learn more. It may involve sending one's email address to you as a means of entering a mailing list.

These four parts will create a consistent arrangement of content. This in turn establishes a smarter approach when used well enough.
Of course, the length of each section will vary. You should keep the introduction and closing sections short while the body is a little longer. The approximate length of each one should be chosen based on the total word count that you want to use. This leads to the next section.

Use Fewer Words At a Time

You might be enticed to use plenty of words but you have to be cautious when marketing yourself. You don't want to force the reader to spend more time looking at your stuff.
You should use about 400 to 600 words of content at the most when marketing yourself. The key is to not only be concise but also simple enough to where you can get your content out in as few words as possible.
Using fewer words especially causes people to think about what else you have to share. You can always reserve some of the more detailed stuff on different parts of your website.
The call to action can also be used to let someone know there's more for you to talk about. This section will let someone know where to go when looking to learn more about whatever it is you have to offer.

Give People a Sense Of What You Do Early

You cannot afford to just let people read on and see what you do without giving them a good idea of this first. You have to let people understand what you are doing as early as possible.
Your content must be organized to where you give your readers an idea of what they are going to look at within the first five to ten seconds of reading your work. This lets people understand

Set Up Connections

Connections must be organized to make it easier for content to be easier for people to figure out. You must set up content in your work based on how it can link up to different ideas.
You'll have to consider what your reader might be thinking about while then organizing that content as needed. Establishing a stronger setup will certainly do well if used properly.
Analogies may be added when you're trying to create connections. Analogies are often used to help you share information with other people in ways that they can understand them.

The types of analogies that you can use will vary based on your subject matter. Be sure to think about your audience and determine what content is easy for the people to understand and follow. This is to make the content you have easily to figure out.

Be To the Point

This rule of thumb for creating content is simple but still logical and easy to follow. The content you create must be to the point.
You don't want to dance around the facts. You have to share what you want to say as soon as possible.
You can always add a slight introduction to your work if needed. This could be to get someone in the mood to hear something or to be clear as to what you want to share. However, anything you add must be easy to follow and figure out.

Create Visual Representations

Visual representations can entail lots of things. They can especially simplify the data you're trying to share.
Such representations include the following:
- Pictures of whatever you want to highlight

- Videos showcasing processes or services you have

- Infographics that organize your data in a unique manner

- Charts that link certain bits of content together.

- The use of bullets, numbered lists or other things to organize your data; this is especially great if many pieces of content have different points linking to each other

This could be perfect for when you're trying to simplify data. People like it when they can take a look at content that isn't jumbled up or all around the place.

In addition, it is often easier to explain things by using pictures or videos. A text-based description of something might be too complicated or difficult to figure out.

You have to establish some great visual representations of anything you want to share in your campaign. There are many great points that should be used when making a great visual representation.

Adding Pictures

Pictures are perfect for how they illustrate many ideas and make it easier for people to understand what you've got to offer. However, you should add pictures in a sensible manner so it won't be too complicated or tough to use. You should add your pictures with care without being too complicated or otherwise challenging for you to use. There are many good tips to use when adding pictures:

- Choose pictures that are clear and sensible. Don't use anything that is overly jumbled or complicated.

- Place your pictures in spots that break up the text. It's easier to read content when it isn't jumbled all around the place.

- Keep your pictures from being too big. You don't want to make pictures cloud up much of the content. The text will still be important and should be used alongside the pictures.

- Any pictures you add should be relevant to the content you are adding to your work. You should avoid using anything that has imagery that might not be sensible when compared with other stuff on your work.

These are smart options for you to use when trying to get your content out there. These options will help you make the most out of anything you have to manage.

Chapter 5 – Marketing Avenues

Knowing what content you want to work with can make a difference when it comes to marketing your work. The ways how you're going to get that information out to people can especially make a difference.

There are many types of content marketing materials that you can use when promoting your business. You must choose an option that is sensible for your demands and offers visitors the information that they crave.

The options here are actually relatively varied and can include ones that are easy to share. This makes for different solutions that can make things right and easy to follow.

Website

The best way to use content marketing is to use your own website. You can always add articles or new detailed bits of content relating to your business on your website.

Considering how the online world is a popular place to share data at, it is a necessity to get your work out online. This is to not only get it out there but to make it easier for people to share that content.

There are many things you can do in particular:
- Create PDFs or other downloadable files on your website and allow people to

download them and share them with others.

- Set up a brochure-style design for your site.

- Make your content as interactive as possible. Establish several sections to discuss as many smaller bits of content as possible.

- Prepare a series of social media buttons around your page. These will let users share your content on a variety of social media sites.

Blogging

A blog is like a website but it clearly doesn't have as many features. That is, it just lists information on things you are posting right now. People can search through a blog and sort topics by categories that you post up too.
A blog is perfect for a variety of purposes:
- Your blog can be linked up to a website you run. This in turn increases the reliable links and content on your site.

- It's often easier to post extended forms of data on a blog.

- Many categories can be used in your blog. These can be listed on the top or bottom parts of your blog posts. Visitors can sort through your content by clicking on different categories on your site.

Direct Mail

Many people assume that direct mail is a dead art form, what with so many people sending things online. However, direct mail is still a very popular option for you to look at.
Think about the mail you might get these days. Have you ever gotten a flyer from a local business in your mailbox? Maybe you got one of those envelopes that offers a series of small ads for various services in your area with some coupons on some of them.
Direct mail is perfect for your content marketing purposes for many reasons:

- It shows how dedicated you are to marketing yourself. It might be easier for people to take your work seriously if you are promoting your work in person with print materials.

- This also highlights the local nature of whatever you have to offer. People are often willing to do business with local entities. They think that they are more trustworthy.

- Your brand may also be easier to notice through a direct mail posting. This comes as you can create a print document that highlights everything your business has to offer.

Social Media

More people are on social media networks than ever before these days. You can always go on social media to share content with other people. To do this, you can post new content and add video or picture files related to it. This can be done a few times in a week.
Best of all, you don't have to spend too much time getting your social media info out there. Social media posts can typically run for a short period and won't entail too much junk getting in the way.

Of course, people can also share the content in your postings online. They can forward whatever you have posted to a variety of places. This allows your content to be easier for people to read and use.

There are some tips to use when getting social media to work for your content marketing plans:

- Avoid adding far too many posts in a week. About three to four posts should be good enough each week.

- Don't go into your history far too often. Leave the content relating to your history on your website.

- Allow people to respond to your social media posts. Let them leave comments or replies. It shows that you're willing to hear what they have to say.

- Try and respond to messages if possible. This shows that you are hearing people and that you are willing to clarify anything that people might be confused about.

Social media will certainly be perfect for your content marketing plans. Spend some time with this each day to see what you can do. It is all about getting in touch with people through some rather popular methods of interaction.

Sharing Images

Images can always be great for when you're trying to share information on your company. Images can be paired with important keywords relating to your business and the content of the image.

A great process for sharing images will certainly do well for your requirements. You can share images on Instagram or Pinterest right now. You should look carefully to see what you are getting out of the process of using these image sites.

- Add pictures to your Instagram or Pinterest site three or four times in a week.

- Use keywords that are relevant to the image. Make sure they are consistent all around your account.

- Work with pictures that deal with whatever you sell. This helps people see that you know what you have to offer.

- Take in pictures of the more recent events in your business and post them online. These include pictures of a recent business meeting, community event, product launch or anything else that might have taken place in your business.

Sharing images shows that you have proof over what you've got to offer. It also places an emphasis on how active your business is in terms of what it is doing. This in turn establishes a better organization in terms of what you want to share with the world.

Using Email the Right Way

It is true that you can always use emails to market yourself to other people. Email newsletters are perfect for when you're trying to market yourself and your content.

Email is easy to access from anywhere provided that an online connection is available. Also, email allows you to be as brief or detailed as you desire.

In addition, you may get access to plenty of leads when you use email. This can come from people not only forwarding your work to others but also from people signing up for emails through a mailing list on your website.

You must be cautious when using email for your content marketing needs. Several things must be done to make your content work well.

- Don't send far too many emails. Sending emails once a week or every two weeks is enough. It makes your emails more exciting. More importantly, it ensures that your emails won't be caught by anyone's spam server.

- Keep your messages short and brief. People who read emails will want to go through them quickly as they might be dealing with loads of them at a given time.

- Place more of an emphasis on new content and what you want to share with your readers. You don't have to go through your background when making emails. The people who are reading them probably know about your business already and don't need a backstory.

The marketing avenues you have for your content marketing needs are certainly amazing. You must think carefully about what you're going to get out of this.

Chapter 6 – Key Pointers For Marketing

The marketing avenues that you just read about are certainly worth using. However, you have to do more than just use the right spots for marketing. You have to also watch out for how you do it.

As you read in the last chapter, you have to keep posting things on a regular basis without being too complicated or busy. However, you should do plenty of additional things to make your work ready and useful.

Understand Your Audience

As great as it can be for you to work with marketing plans, you have to see who your target audience is. The problem with marketing is that it is often a challenge for you to try and get your content out to people who will actually understand it.

You might want to consider your audience to see what social media methods you should use or what other methods are needed. A direct mail process may work well if you have an older audience. A program like Snapchat may be better if your target audience is younger.

Think about what people will reach you with. This is to help you get more out of your plans.

Focus On One Channel At a Time

Content marketing works best when you run with one channel at a time. You don't want to get into a plan that is jumbled or complicated. Choose one channel to build your program on. By using one channel, you can develop a content marketing plan that is carefully organized. After establishing one channel, you can get to the next. This is provided that the first channel is easy to maintain and isn't too complicated.

Keep a Smart Schedule

The next tip is to set up a schedule that is easy to control and won't be too complicated. The process should entail enough help for making it easier for you to create a good habit of managing a better schedule.

Prepare your posts by scheduling them to come at particular times of the day or week. Try and keep that schedule consistent if possible. Make sure it's also a schedule that you can easily follow.

You must keep the schedule working well so it won't be harder to use than necessary. See that you can meet it over the course of a few weeks before you go too far in the process.

A great schedule will make it so your readers will know what to expect. They will see that you're reliable and that you've got new bits of content to share on a regular basis.

This in turn leads to more referrals. This makes it easier for people to grow well and make it work right.

Remember to take a look at what you're going to get out of your marketing plans. You must see that your plans are managed properly enough to be sensible and easy to follow.

Chapter 7 – Creating a Call to Action

Content marketing should involve a call to action in some way. This can come in many forms:

- It can tell people to buy something from you.

- It can tell them to go somewhere to learn more about something.

- You can even have them send information to you to get access to more content.

A great call to action will provide you with more data relating to your visitors. This in turn makes it easier for you to have more content on hand. The call to action should be organized with several critical steps in mind.
1. Make your words compelling.

A great call to action in your content marketing campaign will feature content that is relevant to whatever you want to talk about. It will help people understand how important what you are offering is and that they need to act upon what you are offering to them right now.
2. Create a series of triggers.

Triggers may be added to your call to action to reinforce a decision. Triggers are often used to make your content more enticing.

Triggers can include things like customer reviews, guarantees, benefits relating to what you are marketing and so forth. These are all last minute offers that you can make to show that you are serious about whatever you have to share.

3. Make the call simple.

Your reader will have already taken a look at lots of content in your work. You have to keep the call to action simple so the reader will want to side with you. The call should be organized to where it is brief without forcing anyone to add more content or an extra effort.

4. Keep people from being distracted.

Distractions in the call to action can really hurt its chances. Distractions often entail your content being jumbled with more pictures, different graphics or added content you never bothered to talk about.

Keep the call to action area clear and simple. Allow it to where nothing distracting will get in the way. This in turn makes the content easy to follow.

As you use these pointers, your call to action will become memorable and easy to use. Readers will want to do business with you and get more out of your content.

Don't Forget Social Sharing Buttons

This pointer is loosely related to your call to action but it is just as important. You have to add social sharing buttons to the bottom part of your website. This is to let people sent your work to others through many social media outlets. This is great for cases where you have lots of content to share and you want people to pay attention to it.

You will typically have to add some kind of social media plugin onto your content if you're using this online. This will entail icons that show many different social media services. Using the right icons can be important as it shows that people can share your content with more through many methods.

For print content, you can always list information on your social media handles somewhere in your work. This can be around the call to action. This lets people get to your all to action as they might see fit.

Make sure anything relating to social sharing is suitable. You might not benefit from sharing information about a Google Plus account if you don't have one or the one you have isn't being interacted with all that much. Think about how you're sharing your buttons and use points that you know are easy to handle.

Remember that the call to action for your content marketing plans is very important. It must be organized to where people will pay attention to what you have to offer. This in turn makes your content easier to run with.

Chapter 8 – Additional Tips

The points you have read about in this guide should be perfect for your content marketing needs. There are plenty of added tips that you must follow if you want to make your content marketing plans really do well for you.

Place a Local Focus

In most cases your content is going to be read by people who are closer to you. That is, it might be read by those who want to learn more about a business you run in a local area.

You must have a local focus on your work to make it stand out. Show the people reading your work that you understand whatever it is that you want to share with them.

A local approach may entail talking about things in your area or why your product or service fits the needs of people living in that area. Talk about what people in your area can get out of something and they will see that you understand the demands they have for products or services in different forms.

Reply To Messages Often

You have to be interactive when sharing information with other people. Sending out messages to people is great but it is even better to send messages to people who want more out of you.

You should get messages from others whether it comes from emails, phone calls, social media postings or more. Make sure you respond to them as needed.

Responses can vary based on what you are doing. You might reply to messages by simply thanking someone for sending something. You might also reply by clearing up something that a customer has a concern over. This can include a message that might be detailed or complicated and requires an answer in some way.

You must reply to your messages often so you can show that you care about the needs that individuals have. This is especially given that you don't want people to be confused in some way. Answering questions helps to show that you know what you are talking about and that you want to help people.

Think About Search Intentions

Coming up with the right keywords is always good to do. It helps you think about what people might look for. But what about the intentions people have when searching for you?

A person might put in a particular keyword but there might be a specific reason for it. A person could search for something like "fixing a car" but it might be for something very specific. A person might want to fix a very particular part of a car.

You should think about what people might search for and why they would search for it when coming across keywords for your content marketing campaign. Feel free to enter in a keyword on a search engine and see what related results might come about. This can help you see what you should be adding to your content.

Use Analytics Programs

Sometimes analytics programs can make a difference when you're trying to promote your work. These help you to see who is using your programs and how people are interacting with you.

An analytics program can help you get the most out of the content you're using. A program like Google Analytics lets you take a closer look at how people access your content based on the keywords they search for, the links they reach your content through and so forth.

A good program can help you prepare your future plans for running your campaign. It lets you see what is working and if you need to change things based on what people are getting into.

Conclusion

Content marketing can be perfect for when you're looking to make your work visible and to help people see what makes your business special. Using it right is important to consider as you need to make sure your work is visible and useful to more people.

Be careful when marketing your content. Make sure it is organized well and that you know how to come up with ideas.

Figuring out how you're going to share those ideas will certainly be important to see as well. You should share your content through many methods while also being careful when managing your content.

The process for using content marketing isn't as hard to manage as you might think. This process will do well for your demands so you'll have an easier time highlighting your content.

Good luck with your plans for running a content marketing program. You will certainly be impressed at how well your content can work for you when you're trying to grow your business.

www.ingramcontent.com/pod-product-compliance
Lightning Source LLC
Chambersburg PA
CBHW070405190526
45169CB00003B/1117